Concerning the Birth of Christ

A Discussion of the Timing of Christ's Birth

By: Ben Tripp M. A. Sc., P. Eng.
Cover: Carolyn Tripp B. A.

2

References have been included. A bracketed number will indicate the reference that was used. For example (12) will refer to reference number 12. Any misinterpretation of any of these references must be taken as a shortcoming of the author and him alone. Otherwise it is his hope that the following discussion will be found helpful to all who read it.

ISBN 978-0-9936349-5-6   Book
ISBN 978-1-7751150-2-1   Electronic Book

Other books by the same author:

1,   The Window of Life
       A Theory of the Earth Based on Asteroid Impact
2,   Elements of Providence during the Genesis Flood
3,   Fairytales for Adults
       Theories of the Earth in Disarray
4,   The Asteroid Theory of the Flood and the Ice Age
       The necessity and sufficiency of an asteroid shower to cause an ice age
5,   The non-Myths of the Bible
       The correlation between Scriptural chronology and nature

Forthcoming books by the same author:

1,   The Impossibility of Extraterrestrial Life
2,   Stepping the Mast

       (more info at http://benatripp.wix.com/window-of-life)

4

This work is dedicated to my family

To my dear wife:
Judith Anne
The love of my life

To my children:
Bryan, Rebecca, Daniel and Carolyn
The great blessing of my life

To my dear grandchildren:
Evelyn, Ayla, Zoe, Izzy and Ben

And to my bonus children:
Andrea and Adrian

May this humble epistle assist them in their search for truth.

About the Author: Ben earned both Bachelor's and Master's degrees from the University of Waterloo, Waterloo, Ontario. A consulting engineer with a master's degree in engineering responsible for the design of various test rigs for the CanadArm, controls for large optical telescopes, heavy water plants, wind tunnels and industrial machinery. Other projects include the development of a novel geothermal heat-pump and scrap tire recycling apparatus. The present project is the result of research through numerous articles and books including an effort to sort out the peculiarities and relationships between the ancient Roman calendar and our modern calendar.

...

6

Table of Contents   Page

8

1,0 Foreword

Various discussions concerning just when Christ was born have taken place over the years and have included ideas which do not properly recognize either the facts of history or the realities of science. The most glaring example concerns the Christmas Star. The Bible talks about a star being involved in the birth event and various efforts have been made to match this star to some astronomical event. In so doing inappropriate conclusions have been reached.

If the matter is approached from a 'natural lights-in-the-sky' perspective, there are only a few possible types of events that can be considered. These include:

- a. Nova
- b. Supernova
- c. Comet
- d. Asteroid
- e. Conjunction
- f. Meteorite
- g. Aurora Borealis (Northern Lights)
- h. Noctilucent Clouds (Night-shining clouds)
- i. Ball lightning

In the Bible (17) the description of the phenomenon includes;

- I. "... we have seen His star in the east."
- II. "... what time the star appeared."
- III. "... the star which they saw in the east went before them till it came and stood over where the young child was."
- IV. "When they saw the star they rejoiced with exceeding great joy."

Quotation III indicates that the observers of the star were in Jerusalem at that particular time and that it led them straight to Bethlehem – to an exact location, a house. Any phenomenon above atmospheric level could not have done this. It simply would not have been possible for something that was high enough to be out of the atmosphere to distinguish between the location of Jerusalem and Bethlehem because these two locations are too close together. Therefore, the phenomenon had to have been quite low down in the atmosphere which particular requirement rules out a, b, c, d and e.

Both noctilucent clouds and meteorites are atmospheric events. Meteorites move very quickly. However, quotation I and III require more time than a meteorite would have allowed so it could not have been a meteorite. Noctilucent clouds are an atmospheric phenomenon and they do not move quickly. In fact, they hardly move at all but they are spread out very thin and are barely visible. (Actually noctilucent clouds only appeared very recently - in fact about two years after the Krakatoa explosion in Indonesia in 1883. While there might have been such clouds in ancient time, there is simply no record of them. Noctilucent clouds are understood to be water droplets trapped high in the atmosphere above a layer of atmosphere that is slightly warmer. Therefore they cannot descend and are likely to be up there for a very long time.)

The Aurora Borealis (i.e. northern lights) commonly put on spectacular light shows in the atmosphere. They present in a variety of colors as they shimmer and dance across the sky in totally unpredictable patterns. However, they occur many times every year and are never observed to focus into a tight stationary pattern at any particular location. In order to meet the criteria of the report, tight focus, stationary positioning (at least for more than a few minutes) and rarity of occurrence are all absolutely necessary.

Ball Lightning meets the criteria of being tightly focused because the phenomenon presents as a glowing sphere several inches in diameter. The actual substance of these balls is thought to consist of atoms partially stripped of their normal complement of electrons. They do become momentarily stationary on occasion but most of the time they are on the move and commonly moving at significant speed. They might occur at any elevation from ground level to well up in the atmosphere as high as the more common types of lightning occur. Could a ball lightning event develop far to the east of Jerusalem, redevelop several weeks later between Jerusalem and Bethlehem and then drift over to Bethlehem at a speed commensurate with the movement of a group of camels? Then, could it hover over one particular well-defined location (i.e. a house) long enough for the camels to catch up? While ball lightning is certainly not very well understood, meeting such a criteria does not seem very likely.

Therefore the result of this very brief investigation is that there isn't any particular atmospheric or above-atmospheric event that can explain the Christmas Star. In spite of this however one of the above possibilities deserves further comment. While ruled out previously because of altitude, conjunctions have never-the-less been occasionally advanced to explain the Christmas Star.

Conjunctions are events in the Solar System where, from the viewpoint of Earth, two or more planets line up in the sky. While Venus has the brightness of a bright white star, the others do not. Mars shows as a medium brightness red star and Jupiter and Saturn are hardly visible to the untrained eye. However the planets do line up from time to time and if they formed a tight grouping it would have the brightness of a bright star. However, they very seldom get close enough together to show as a single unit. The term conjunction is actually applied quite loosely and is commonly used to describe a grouping of planets in the night sky even if they are several degrees apart. In such a case, the apparent brightness of the group would not be any brighter than the planet Venus on its own.

The final reason that conjunctions do not provide a reasonable explanation is that there wasn't (from the point of view of the necessary lines of reasoning discussed below), one near the time of Christ's birth. The closest one that is occasionally mentioned occurred in 7 BCE, which will be seen to be several years too soon. Consequently it is simply too remote in time to be of interest. Further, we understand that it wasn't really a very tight formation. Therefore a conjunction cannot be used as a primary time reference for the birth of Christ. However, if there had been a tight conjunction closer to the birth-time, it might have been supportive of the other lines of reasoning.

12

2,0   Introduction

For several hundred years prior to the time of Christ as well as for several hundred years thereafter the Roman calendar was in use. While it was in widespread use it was never imposed and so there were actually several other calendars in use as well. In some cases even cities had their own calendar. Fortunately the existence of other calendars does not affect our present discussion because the Roman calendar was the one that was in widespread use across the lands at the eastern end of the Mediterranean Sea - the area involved in this particular discussion.

It wasn't until several hundred years after the time of Christ that the present or 'Christian' calendar came into use. Dionysius Exiguus was a Christian scholar and he is credited with introducing the idea of having a calendar referenced to the birth of Christ. This development occurred in 525 AD (2) but it wasn't until the 8th century that the idea was introduced into historical writings and that Charles the Great (Charlemagne) promoted its more widespread use. All events prior to that time have been superimposed onto the Christian calendar after the fact. For the most part this has worked all right but for BCE dates a problem was introduced which remains to this day. More comment will be offered concerning the calendar in the discussion to follow.

When Dionysius introduced the Christian calendar, he placed its starting time at 753 AUC because he thought that was the year that Christ was born.(2) While we understand now that the starting date should have been a little earlier, the calendar will never be changed. Once historical events were identified on the calendar it would have become totally impossible to change them – partly because of the inconvenience and partly because of the lack of any benefit from so doing. The calendar is now used throughout most of the world and it is expected that it will remain in use indefinitely.

AUC is the designation for the ancient Roman calendar and it is the short form for either 'ab urba condita' or 'anno urbis conditae' both of which mean: The year of the founding of the city. (7)

Throughout this discussion the following understanding will be applied. When the word year is followed by a number, we are referring to a date. For example, 'the year 1955' refers to the calendar year 1955 and to something that happened that year. When the word year is preceded by a number, we are referring to a period of time. An example of this second arrangement is '1255 years'. Clearly, a span of 1255 years is involved and the time has not been specified. With this understanding we are in a position to ask the first question.

3,0   Question Number 1
       Did the Christian Era begin at the time zero?

In order to deal with this question let us consider the following approach. At the end of 1999 was it 2000 years since the beginning of the present, Christian or modern era or was it only 1999 years? Did the first year of the modern calendar run from time zero to the beginning of year one or from the beginning of year one to the beginning of year two? Is the first year equivalent to year one or is the second year equivalent to year one?

3,1   The Destruction of the Temple

On January 1st of 70 AD it was 70 years after Jan 1^{St} of the first year having the AD designation. When 70 years are subtracted from the year 823 AUC, the result is 753 AUC. If we subtract (or go back in time), we arrive at Jan. 1st 753 AUC. Since 70 full years have been subtracted we are back at Jan. 1ST, 0 AD, which would be the beginning or starting time for the present era. Then, the year which follows this starting time would be the first year of the present era. On the calendar it would necessarily be identified as the year 0 and not the year 1.

The year zero was the subject of a lot of controversy around the beginning of the 21st century with some people taking the position that there was no such thing. However there was a year zero and necessarily so or the present era would be missing a year and it would not include 2014 plus years. This is clearly shown in the charts for eclipses of the Moon as listed on the NASA website. However, the same cannot be said for the previous era as can also be seen from these same charts. More will be said on this point as the present discussion proceeds.

To review, after 70 years from the starting time has passed, we would arrive at Jan. 1st of the 71st year of the present era. It is equivalent and proper to also say we are at Jan 1st of the year 70 AD. With reference back to the introduction we can see that '71st year' is referring to a very particular year (or time) in history whereas '70 years' is referring to a span of time.

The choice of 70 for the above discussion has not arbitrary because it was during the year 70 AD, (actually 70 years 7 months and 5 days from the beginning of the present era) that the temple in Jerusalem was destroyed. (1) Neither was the year 823 AUC chosen arbitrarily because that year on the Roman calendar was the same year as the year 70 on the present calendar. (1)

If the declaration of Dionysius (2) was intended to mean that the year 753 would be the first year of the Christian or modern calendar, this would co-ordinate with and reinforce these deductions. However, if either reference 1 or reference 2 is incorrect, the conclusion that the beginning of the year 753 would be the beginning of the Christian calendar is not valid. The present discussion will proceed with the assumption that both references are correct.

3,2   The Founding of Rome

Rome was founded 753 years, 7 months and 8 days prior to the beginning of the year 753 AUC. (3) This corroborates having the beginning of the year 753 AUC as the starting time for the present era. Whether Rome was founded at that particular ancient time or not is immaterial. It is simply that the terminology is consistent in placing the beginning of the year 753 coincident with the beginning of the year 0 AD of the Common (i.e. present) Era.

It has been declared that the Romans did not have a zero in their system of numbers and neither did the people of Dionysius' time (which was several hundred years later). Therefore there could not have been a year zero. Unfortunately for that viewpoint, what the Romans thought about the idea of zero is of no relevance whatsoever. Neither did they know about our present calendar or the solar system or McDonald's hamburgers.

That first year was the year zero just the same as a person's age during the first year of life is 0 and halfway through the tenth year of their life, they are 9 years and 6 months old. A baby would never be declared to have an age 0. During the first year, its age would be given in months and weeks or possibly even days. Then after it had lived for a year it would be referred to as being one year and so many months or weeks old. In fact, all during the year that the baby was 1, it would actually be 1 plus some other amount of time up to 12 months. Similarly, all during the year that it was 2, it would actually be 2 plus some additional continually-changing amount of time up to 12 months.

The first year of the modern era calendar is equivalent to the 754th year (i.e. the year 753 AUC) of the Roman calendar That year ran from the end of the 753rd year to the end of the 754th year. During that year it was 753 years plus, since Rome was thought to have been founded.

The first year of the modern era ran from time zero for a period of 12 months to the end of that first year. During the second year, the date was year 1 plus some number of months from 0 to 12. During the first year, the date was simply some number of months - the same that it is during the first year of a person's life. For example, the birth date for a child born on the 23rd of March of that second year would be Mar. 23, 1. Of course this calendar wasn't the least bit unusual or confusing for anybody at that time because it was not in use at that time. It only came into use several hundred years later necessitating that all dates in other calendars or even those not yet assigned, be superimposed onto this new (Christian) calendar.

Therefore it may be concluded that it was 2000 years from the beginning of the present era to the end of the year 1999. After the beginning of the year 2000 it was more than 2000 years since the beginning of the present era.

18

4,0   Question Number 2
      When did Herod the Great die?

The date for the birth of Christ is closely related to the date for the death of
Herod the Great because it is evident from scripture (17) that Jesus was born a
short period of time prior to the death of Herod. Therefore by identifying the time
of Herod's death, the time of the birth of Christ is closely identified.

4,1   The Rule of Herod

If the Christian calendar started 70 years and 7 months before the Temple was
destroyed, then there are no missing years from the calendar from the present
era. Herod the Great died shortly before Passover, 750 AUC. (22) Passover that
year was April 12. (22) Further, it was 107 years from the beginning of Herod's
rule until the destruction of the Temple. (5) Herod's rule would therefore have
begun 107 years (plus or minus up to six months) minus 70 years and 7 months
prior to the start of the Common Era. This works out to be 36 years and 5 months
(plus or minus up to six months) prior to the start of the Common Era. Since he
reigned for 34 years, (4) he must have died about 2 years and 5 months (plus or
minus six months) prior to the start of the Common Era. While Josephus'
reference to years (i.e. reference 5) does not give years and months, it is
reasonable to assume that the actual period of time involved would be within six
months of the number of years stated.

4,2   The Death of Herod

The year 823 AUC is the same as the year 70 CE. (1) From the above discussion we
learned that there are no missing years from the Common Era calendar, (i.e. that
the year zero is not missing) placing the beginning of the Christian calendar at the
beginning of 753 AUC. The author of Life and Times is quite adamant that Herod
died in 750 AUC. (22) His conclusion places the year 750 AUC equivalent with the
third year BCE and places the death of Herod about 2 years and 9 months prior to
the start of the Common Era or prior to zero time.

Further, if Dionysius intension, as stated in reference 2, was that the year 753 AUC was the first year of the Christian calendar, this together with the comment in the Enclyclopedia Britannia (reference 7) also places the death of Herod about 2 years and 9 months prior to the Common Era.

The death of Herod followed an eclipse of the Moon by an unknown period (18) which, from the context of this reference, appears to have been several days. If this unknown period was, for example, two weeks, the death of Herod would have been a little less than 2 years and 9 months prior to zero time.

4,3   Summary

From the comments of Josephus', the death of Herod would have been about 2 years and 5 months prior to the start of the Common Era. However the variance included is plus or minus six months. The eclipse of the Moon places his death about 2 years and 9 months prior to the Common Era. The historical comments included in the encyclopedia also indicate about the same time as does the comments in the Life and Times reference.

5,0   Question Number 3

What time of year was Christ born?

5,1   The Death of Herod the Great

The death of Herod was near the end of March of 750 AUC. (7) When the Wise Men visited Herod, he was at Jerusalem (17) which therefore must have been prior to his treatment-seeking journey east. The amount of time after Herod left Jerusalem and before he died is not known but it was certainly more than the 5 days between Antipater's death and his death (24) and would have been at least several more days or even weeks. The Wise Men visited Herod in Jerusalem, went to Bethlehem and then headed home another way to avoid Herod. (9) Immediately after that, Joseph left for Egypt. Sometime after his meeting with the Wise Men, Herod journeyed east of the Jordan seeking treatment for his debilitating illness (25) and then returned to Jericho, caused the death of Antipater and then died himself 5 days later. (24)

Prior to the visit of the Wise Men, Joseph, Mary and Jesus were in Jerusalem unmolested and went to the Temple for recognition after the purification period which was 41 days (23) following the birth of Jesus. While Herod might have been in Jerusalem at that time he was apparently unaware either of Jesus presence in the city or of the recognition which was being given to Him at the Temple.

The Wise Men traveled from the east (It is suspected that they came from Babylon or near Babylon) and the time of travel is not given but would normally take several weeks. It would be reasonable to assume that they started west soon after seeing the 'star'. Since they arrived after Mary and Joseph had left Jerusalem following their Temple visit, their travel time was probably coincident with and a little more than the purification time.

Therefore between Jesus birth and Herod's death, there are several periods of interest including:

a.   41 days for purification period

b. Time between the end of the purification period and the visit of Wise Men

c. The period of time from the visit of the Wise Men until Herod ordered Antipater's death.

d. Antipater's death to Herod's death 5 days

Therefore the birth of Christ would not have been later than 46 days (i.e. 41 plus 5 from a. and d.) plus the two unknown periods (i.e. b. and c.) prior to Herod's earliest possible death.

5,2   The Beginning of Jesus' Ministry

When Jesus began His ministry He was about 30 years old. (28) The age 30 was recognized as an important age of maturity implying that Jesus was at least 30 but not yet 31. From other sources 'about 30' means 'very close to 30'. Herein it will be taken to mean closer to 30 than 31. John began to minister very shortly before this when Tiberius was in the 15th year of his reign. (26) Further, Augustus enabled Tiberius to co-reign with him starting on January 16, 13 CE. (29) Therefore Jesus lived for at least 14+ years (i.e. Tiberius' reign) plus 13 years and 16 days (i.e. Augustus reign) during the present era. Therefore He lived for a total of 27 years and 16 days as well as two unknown periods during the present era. The first unknown period is the portion of the 15th year of Tiberius. The second unknown period is the time between the beginning of John's ministry and the beginning of Jesus' ministry.

Therefore, to determine the portion of His life that was lived during the previous era, the 30+ years is subtracted from the 27 years and 16 days and the two unknown periods. This results in 3 years minus 16 days and places the birth of Jesus about mid-January during the third year of the previous era. The unknown periods are offsetting. The unknown portion of His 31st year places His birth earlier by the same amount because a greater amount of time must be subtracted. If, for example, Jesus' age at the beginning of His ministry was 30 years and 3 months, the time of birth would be three months earlier or about mid-October of the fourth year before the present era. But if Tiberius was 2 months into his 15th year, we arrive back at mid-December of the fourth year BCE. The maximum deviation occurs earlier if:

i.   Tiberius was barely into his 15th year.

ii.   Jesus was 3 months into His 31ˢᵗ year. (Assuming that 3 months is the maximum deviation from His 30ᵗʰ birthday)
iii.   There was zero time between the beginnings of the two ministries.

This would place the birth 3 months earlier at mid-October of the fourth year BCE. The maximum deviation later occurs if:

i.   Tiberius was well into his 15ᵗʰ year. (i.e. 10 months)
ii.   Jesus was at the very beginning of His 31ˢᵗ year.
iii.   There was a delay between the beginnings of the two ministries. (i.e. one month)

In this case, the deviation would be 11 months later to mid-December of the third year BCE.
Example calculation:

   Earliest: (27 years + 16 days) - (30 years + 2 months) = - (3 years + 1 ½ months)
From this calculation the time of birth would have been mid-November during the fourth year BCE.

   Latest: (27 years + 16 days + 1 month + 10 months) – (30 years) = - (2 years + 14 days)
From this second calculation the time of birth would have been mid-December of the third year BCE.

5,3   The Priest Named Zacharias

Zacharias belonged to the priestly division of Abijah. (14) The temple was destroyed on the 9-10 of Ab when the course of Jehoiarib was on duty. (1) By counting backwards, the course of Abijah would have been on duty from 2ⁿᵈ to 9ᵗʰ of October during the year 748 AUC. (15) Apparently each course served for two weeks every year. (30) Further it is thought that they served for a one week period every six months. (31) Sometime after Zechariah returned home his wife Elizabeth became pregnant. (16) When Elizabeth was in her sixth month of pregnancy, the angel of the Lord appeared to Mary and shortly thereafter she went to visit her cousin Elizabeth. (32)

Therefore there are several reasonably well-defined periods of time involved which will enable the time of the birth of Jesus to be approximated. Between the end of Zechariah's priestly duty and the birth of Jesus, the following times are involved.

> A. Unknown time until Elizabeth became pregnant.
>
> B. Five months of Elizabeth's pregnancy.
>
> C. Unknown portion of the sixth month of Elizabeth's pregnancy
>
> D. The term of Mary's pregnancy.

The shortest expected time for these periods of time is 0 + 5 + 0 + 9 months, assuming that Mary's pregnancy went full term. This calculation would take us forward 14 months from the end of Zechariah's period of duty to Dec. 9 of the year 749 AUC. The two unknown periods add to this time. For example, if Elizabeth was two weeks into her sixth month when Mary visited, the date of the birth of Jesus would have been Dec 23, 749 AUC. Further, if the first of the unknown periods was 2 days, the date for the birth of Jesus would have been Dec 25, 749 AUC.

It is curious that the Jews recognized a fast day on the 9th Tebbeth (December) but a reason was not given. However, 'Jewish chronologists have fixed on that day as that of Christ's birth and it is remarkable that between the years 500 and 816 AD the 9th Tebbeth fell on Dec 25 twelve times.' (33)

5,4   The Shepherds

Shepherds were tending their flocks near Bethlehem the night that Jesus was born. (20) This fact on its own would not be significant but it becomes significant when it is coupled with the observation that shepherds did not pasture their flocks close to Bethlehem all during the year. Bethlehem is located in a semi-desert region adjacent to an actual desert to the east. In order to pasture flocks grass is needed and in order to have grass rainfall is needed. Apparently near Bethlehem rainfall is only sufficient for about three months of the year. Usually the rest of the year flocks must be pastured further away. While rainfall varies

24

from year to year it was generally only sufficient to produce pasture around Bethlehem during December, January and February. (21)

5,5 Summary

In attempting to identify the time of the birth of Jesus, four lines of reasoning have been employed. The first two were singular events that would not have been repeatable. These include the death of Herod and the beginning of Jesus ministry. The third one, Zechariah, would have been repeatable because the priests were on duty every year. The fourth one, the Shepherds would also have been repeatable because the shepherds pastured their flocks near Bethlehem for several months every year up until Passover in the spring. (21) While the third and fourth lines are repeatable, they correlate to the first two with respect to the time of year but not the actual year.

26

6,0   Question Number 1 Revisited.
      Did the Christian Era begin at time zero?

In the above discussion it has been concluded that the birth of Christ was no later than early in the third year before the present era and no earlier than late in the fourth year before the present era. Included in the data which were used to reach this conclusion is the fact that Jesus was in His 31st year when Tiberius was in his 15th year of control. But Tiberius would have been in his 15th year during 27 AD (recall he started to reign with Augustus in Jan. of 13 AD) As before when 27 known years are subtracted from the known date of 27 AD the result is zero. Thus we arrive back at sometime during the first year of the present era which is necessarily the year 0 and not the year 1.

28

7,0   The Missing Year

When dates are given for the BC era, do they count from zero or one? Was the first 12 months of the BC era the first year of that era or year one of that era?

The beginning of Herod's rule was in the year 37 BCE. (10) However, the Temple was destroyed in 823 AUC (1) 102 years after Herod began to reign. (5) This places the beginning of Herod's rule during the 37th year BCE. In this manner, the 37th year is equated with the year 37 BCE.

The death of Augustus occurred in August 14 of 14 AD. (11) This is 14 years and 7 ½ months from zero time (11) The beginning of his rule is given as 43 BCE as well as 57 years prior to August of 14 AD (11) This would place it 42 years and 4 ½ months prior to zero time or during the 43rd year BCE. In this manner the year 43 BCE is equated to the 43rd year BCE. (For clarity, during the Common Era, the year 43 would be recognized as the 44th year just as a person who has passed his 53rd birthday is in his 54th year.)

The above question has therefore been answered and it is clear that there is a year missing from the calendar for dates prior to the Common Era. This conclusion is further reinforced from a review of the tables for lunar eclipses during the first few years of the previous era. (19) A review of these tables makes it clear that the first decade of the previous era only had 9 years in it.

The tables given for lunar eclipses do not include a zero in the previous era. However they do include a zero in the present era. (13) In this manner, the 3rd year BCE is equated with the year 3 BCE as discussed above.

In a discussion accompanying the lunar eclipse tables it is explicitly recognized that a year is missing. 'In this catalog, (i.e. the catalog of the lunar eclipse tables) dates are counted using the astronomical numbering system which recognizes the year 0. Historians should note the numerical difference of one year between astronomical dates and BCE dates. Thus the year 0 corresponds to 1 BCE and the year 100 corresponds to 101 BCE etc.' (12) This situation is illustrated in the time charts in the Appendix. It is readily seen how this situation developed because there would have been an inclination to reckon backwards from the beginning of the first year of the Common Era whereas all reckoning should have been in the direction of time instead. While the dating system would be counting backwards, time would actually have been flowing the other way and this should have been kept in mind. The result of this misstep is simply that the first decade of the previous era only has nine years in it instead of ten.

From this reasoning it can readily be seen how such a situation could have developed. It has nothing whatsoever to do with whether or not the Romans had a zero or did not have a zero. In fact the entire situation developed much more recently and dates for ancient events are still being assigned to the previous era right to the present time. The net result of the above error is that events which occurred during the previous era have been assigned dates which make them appear one year further into the distant past than they are in reality.

8,0   Question Number 4;
      What year was Christ born?

8,1   Lunar Eclipses

Lunar Eclipses are not only useful for identifying the time of year but they also are useful for narrowing down the possible years that Christ could have been born. We understand that a lunar eclipse occurred shortly before the death of Herod the Great. (18) This partial eclipse that occurred during March of the 3rd year BCE supports the conclusion that Herod the Great died that spring. Further, since Christ was born within a few weeks prior to Herod's death, suggesting that he was born late in the 4th year or early in the 3rd year BCE is appropriate. However, we further note that there was also an eclipse of the Moon during March of the previous year. (34) While this raises the possibility that Herod the Great could have died that year the other evidence points to the following year as discussed. However, because this previous eclipse was during the spring as well, it offers a second, albeit more remote, possibility, for which year was involved. Conversely it limits the possible years that Christ could have been born to only two because the eclipses of the previous years are simply too far removed in time when compared to all of the other evidence. When various lines of evidence become supportive of each other any conclusions that are drawn gain more credibility.

8,2   The Death of Herod

The year of the death of Herod the Great is understood to be one of the most well recognized dates in ancient history. (8) The year of Herod's death has been determined to be 750 AUC. (22) However since Herod's death was in the spring (22) and since Christ was born within several weeks prior to this, He would have been born either earlier that year or late in 749 AUC.

8,2   The Roman Rulers

There were only two Roman rulers during the time that Jesus lived. Augustus was ruling from well before Christ was born until Aug. 14, 14 CE. (11) Tiberius began to co-reign with Augustus on Jan. 16, 13 CE (29) and he was in the 15th year of his reign (9) when John the Baptist began his ministry. Jesus began his ministry shortly thereafter when He was about 30 years old. (28,29) Therefore we have the 14 years of Tiberius reign and the 13 years plus 16 days of Augustus' reign coinciding with the ministry of Jesus during the Common Era. This places about 3 years of Jesus life in the previous era and takes us back to the beginning of the 3rd year BCE. As discussed above, the unknowns are offsetting but in any event they do not amount to more than a few weeks at the most. Therefore from the chronology associated with the Roman rulers the birth of Christ would have been either in the 3rd or 4th year BCE.

8,3   Summary

A,   The lunar eclipses indicate either the 3rd or 4th year BCE

B,   The death of Herod indicates the 3rd year BCE.

C,   The Roman ruler's chronology indicates either the 3rd or 4th year BCE

9,0   Conclusion

From the above discussion for the time of year we have:

a. The death of Herod the Great was in late March and the birth of Christ preceded this by several weeks.
b. Reckoning from the beginning of Jesus ministry and including all known possible deviations, the birth of Christ would have been between mid-November and mid-December of the following year.
c. Calculating from the ministry of Zechariah, the birth of Jesus would have been no earlier than Dec. 9 and no later than early January of the following year.
d. The quoted reference indicated that the Shepherds would have been in the fields near Bethlehem during December, January and February.

From the above discussion for the year we have the following;

a. There was a partial lunar eclipse during March of the third year BCE supporting the conclusion that Herod the Great died in the spring of that year.
b. The only other lunar eclipse of particular interest with respect to the year of Christ's birth was the one that occurred during March of the previous year. However this one is more remote in time when the other factors are considered and is therefore of less weight with respect to the final conclusion.
c. The death of Herod was during the year 750 AUC (3rd year BCE).
d. Calculating from the time that the various Roman rulers were in power, the birth of Christ would have been in the 3rd or 4th year BCE.

When both the conclusions for the time of year as well as for the particular year are considered the birth of Christ is concluded to have been no earlier than late in the 4th year BCE (i.e. the year 4 BCE) and no later than early in the 3rdyear BCE (i.e. the year 3 BCE). Further to suggest that it could have been on December 25 of the 4th year BCE is not an exaggeration in the least nor is the suggestion that it was early the following year as observed by certain Christian groups to this day. The Summary Time Chart below shows these relationships.

34

Appendix A

Summary Time Chart
| Jan | Feb | Mar | April | May | June | July | Aug | Sept | Oct | Nov | Dec |

Fourth year BCE (i.e. the year 4 BCE) factors:

Shepherds	xxxxxx
Zechariah	xxxxx
Jesus ministry	xxxxxxxxxxxxxxxx
Herod the Great	xxxxxxxx

Third year BCE (i.e. the year 3 BCE) factors:

xxxxxxxxxxxx	shepherds
xxxxx	Zechariah
xxxxxxxxxxxxxxxxxxxxxxxxxxxxxxxxxxxxxxxxxxxxxxxxxxxxxxxxxx	Jesus' ministry
xxxxxxxxx	Herod the Great

36

Appendix B   Time Chart Number 1

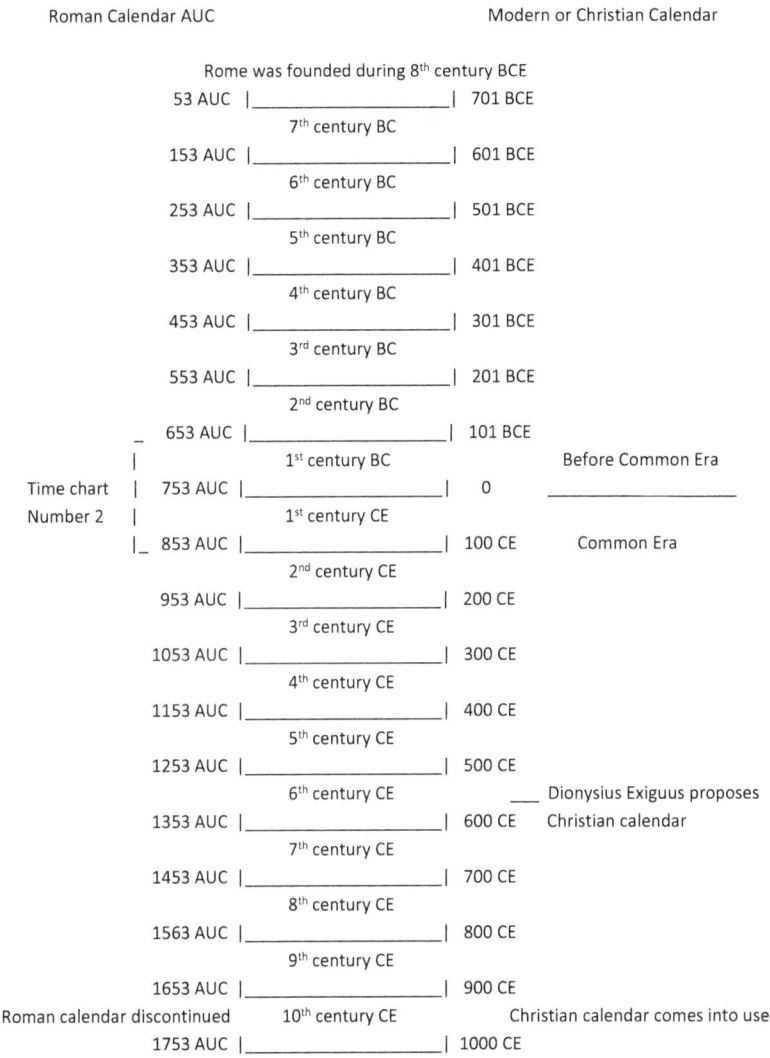

Roman Calendar AUC   Modern or Christian Calendar

Rome was founded during 8th century BCE

| 53 AUC | |_____| | 701 BCE |
7th century BC

| 153 AUC | |_____| | 601 BCE |
6th century BC

| 253 AUC | |_____| | 501 BCE |
5th century BC

| 353 AUC | |_____| | 401 BCE |
4th century BC

| 453 AUC | |_____| | 301 BCE |
3rd century BC

| 553 AUC | |_____| | 201 BCE |
2nd century BC

_   653 AUC | |_____| | 101 BCE
| 1st century BC   Before Common Era

Time chart | 753 AUC | |_____| | 0   _____

Number 2 | 1st century CE

|_ 853 AUC | |_____| | 100 CE   Common Era
2nd century CE

953 AUC | |_____| | 200 CE
3rd century CE

1053 AUC | |_____| | 300 CE
4th century CE

1153 AUC | |_____| | 400 CE
5th century CE

1253 AUC | |_____| | 500 CE
6th century CE   ___ Dionysius Exiguus proposes

1353 AUC | |_____| | 600 CE   Christian calendar
7th century CE

1453 AUC | |_____| | 700 CE
8th century CE

1563 AUC | |_____| | 800 CE
9th century CE

1653 AUC | |_____| | 900 CE

Roman calendar discontinued   10th century CE   Christian calendar comes into use

1753 AUC | |_____| | 1000 CE

38

Appendix C   Time Chart Number 2

Roman Calendar AUC   Modern or Christian Calendar

```
            663 AUC  |_____|  91 BCE
                        9th decade BCE
            673 AUC  |_____|  81 BCE
                        8th decade BCE
            683 AUC  |_____|  71 BCE
                        7th decade BCE
            693 AUC  |_____|  61 BCE
                        6th decade BCE
            703 AUC  |_____|  51 BCE
                        5th decade BCE        ____ Augustus begins to reign
            713 AUC  |_____|  41 BCE         |
      ____                4th decade BCE                  |
   |    723 AUC  |_____|  31 BCE             |
   |                3rd decade BCE                        |     Time of
Time of   |  733 AUC  |_____|  21 BCE        |     Augustus
Herod     |                2nd decade BCE                 |
   |    743 AUC  |_____|  11 BCE             |
   |                1st decade BCE                        | __
   |___ 753 AUC  |_____|  0                  |    | Time chart
   |                1st decade CE                         | __ | number 3
Time of   |  763 AUC  |_____|  10 CE         |
Christ    |                2nd decade CE              ____ | Augustus dies
   |    773 AUC  |_____|  20 CE
   |                3rd decade CE
   |___ 783 AUC  |_____|  30 CE
                        4th decade CE
            793 AUC  |_____|  40 CE
                        5th decade CE
            803 AUC  |_____|  50 CE
                        6th decade CE
            813 AUC  |_____|  60 CE
                        7th decade CE
            823 AUC  |_____|  70 CE  ___ Temple was destroyed
                        8th decade CE
            833 AUC  |_____|  80 CE
                        9th decade CE
```

40

Appendix D   Time Chart Number 3   xx Birth window referencing from shepherds
oo Birth window referencing from Zechariah

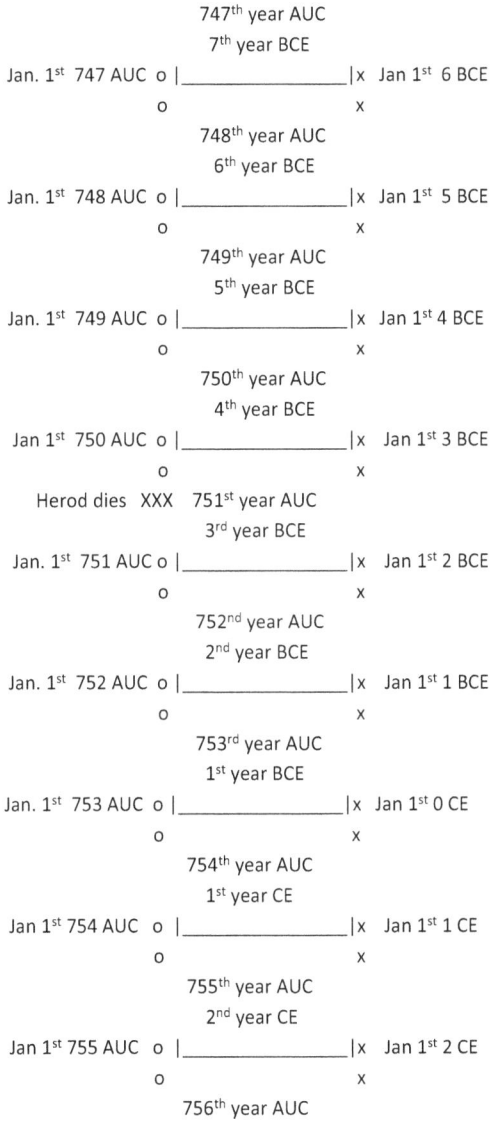

747th year AUC
7th year BCE

Jan. 1st 747 AUC o |_____|x Jan 1st 6 BCE

o   x

748th year AUC
6th year BCE

Jan. 1st 748 AUC o |_____|x Jan 1st 5 BCE

o   x

749th year AUC
5th year BCE

Jan. 1st 749 AUC o |_____|x Jan 1st 4 BCE

o   x

750th year AUC
4th year BCE

Jan 1st 750 AUC o |_____|x Jan 1st 3 BCE

o   x

Herod dies   XXX   751st year AUC
3rd year BCE

Jan. 1st 751 AUC o |_____|x Jan 1st 2 BCE

o   x

752nd year AUC
2nd year BCE

Jan. 1st 752 AUC o |_____|x Jan 1st 1 BCE

o   x

753rd year AUC
1st year BCE

Jan. 1st 753 AUC o |_____|x Jan 1st 0 CE

o   x

754th year AUC
1st year CE

Jan 1st 754 AUC o |_____|x Jan 1st 1 CE

o   x

755th year AUC
2nd year CE

Jan 1st 755 AUC o |_____|x Jan 1st 2 CE

o   x

756th year AUC

Appendix E	References:	Abbreviation
The New Bible Commentary Revised By Guthrie et al		New
The Life and Times of Jesus the Messiah By Edersheim		Life and Times
Funk & Wagnalls New Encyclopedia Edited by Robert S. Phillips		Funk & Wagnalls
Josephus, The Complete Works Translated by William Whiston, A.M.		Josephus
Eclipse Catalog from NASA http://sunearth.gsfc.nasa.gov/eclipse		NASA
Encyclopedia Britannia 1958		En. Br.

44

Appendix F   References by number:

1, The Temple was destroyed on 9-10 Ab of 823 AUC or 5th of Aug. 70 AD.   (Life and Times Vol. 2 p 705)

2, Dionysius Exiguus understood that Christ was born in the year 753 AUC and that the Christian calendar should start that year.   (Funk and Wagnalls Vol. 6 p 272)

3, Rome was founded on April 22, 753 BC.   (Funk and Wagnalls Vol. 6 p 272)

4, Herod the Great ruled for 34 years after the death of Antigonus. (Josephus 17.8.1)

5, It was 107 years from the beginning of Herod's rule until the destruction of the Temple.   (Josephus p 1045)

6, Herod died shortly before Passover which was April 12, 750 AUC. (Life and Times Vol. 1 p 218)

7, Encyclopedia Britannia 1958

8, Life and Times Vol. 2, page 204

9,   Luke 3, verse 1, The Holy Bible, New International Version 1978

10, Herod the Great began to rule in 37 BCE.   (En Br. Vol. 11, p 511)

11, Augustus died on Aug. 14, 14 AD ... on the anniversary of his entrance upon his first consulship 57 years before. (En Br Vol. 2 p 689)

12, NASA

13, The year zero is missing from the lunar eclipse tables for the BC era. (NASA)

14, Zechariah belonged to the priestly division of Abijah.   (Luke 1:5)

15, The course of Abijah would have been on duty from the 2nd to 9th of October during the year 748 AUC. (Life and Times Vol.2 p 705)

16, Sometime after Zechariah returned home, his wife Elizabeth became pregnant with John the Baptist. (Luke 1:24)

17, The Holy Bible, King James Version, St. Matthew, Chapter 2.

18, An eclipse of the Moon occurred shortly before Herod died. (Josephus 17.6.4 (167) 17.8.1 (191))

19,   A partial eclipse of the Moon occurred at 12:10 am on Mar 13, of the third year BCE. (NASA)

20, Shepherds were tending their flocks near Bethlehem the night that Jesus was born. (Luke 2: 8-13)

21,   There is a discussion of rainfall around Bethlehem in Life and Times Vol. 1 p 187 and Vol. 2 p 704.

22,   Herod died between Mar 12, 750 AUC (i.e. eclipse time) and April 12, 750 AUC (i.e. Passover time). (Life and Times Vol. 1, page 218)

23,   Purification period was 41 days. (Life and Times Vol. 1, page 194)

24,   Herod caused the death of Antipater his son, 5 days before he died. (Josephus 17.8.1 (191)) At this time Herod was at his palace in Jericho and was extremely ill. (Josephus 17.6.5 (173))

25,   Immediately prior to this he was east of the Jordan seeking treatment for his extreme illness. (Josephus 17.6.5 (171))

26,   John the Baptist began his ministry during the fifteenth year of Tiberius. (Luke 3:1)

27,   Jesus was baptized shortly thereafter and began his ministry. (Luke 3, 23)

28,   When Jesus began his ministry he was about 30 years old. (Luke 3:23)

29,   Tiberius began to reign with Augustus on Jan. 16, 13 AD. (En Br. Vol2 p 689)

30,   Apparently, each course served for two weeks every year. (NEW page 890)

31,   Further, it is thought that they served for a one week period every six months. (Life and Times Vol. 1 p 135)

32,   When Elizabeth was in her sixth month of pregnancy, the angel of the Lord came to Mary and shortly thereafter she went to visit her cousin Elizabeth. (Luke 1:40)

33,   Life and Times, Vol. 1, page 187

34,   Springtime eclipses of the Moon relevant to the present discussion (NASA)

> A, Mar 2, 2nd year BCE
>
> B, Mar 13, 3rd year BCE
>
> C, Mar 23, 4th year BCE
>
> D, April 4th, 5th year BCE
>
> E, April 14, 6th year BCE